Sir Winston
Churchill
Knew
My Mother

First published in 2006 by Ambit Books,
17 Priory Gardens, London N6 5QY, UK
Publisher: Martin Bax
© 2006 by Satyendra Srivastava
Cover image © 2006 by Vanessa Jackson
The moral rights of the author and artist are asserted in
accordance with the Copyright, Designs and Patent Act, 1988

All rights reserved. No part of this publication may be reproduced,
stored in a retrieval system, or transmitted, in any form or by any means,
electronic, mechanical, photocopying, recording or otherwise without the prior
permission in writing of the publisher.

ISBN 0-900055-09-X

A limited edition (1–25) is available in a slipcase,
signed by author, artist, designer and publisher, at £25.
Order direct from Ambit, 17 Priory Gardens, London N6 5QY, UK

Designed by John Morgan studio
Cover image by Vanessa Jackson
Printed in Great Britain by The Lavenham Press
Distributed by Central Books
The publisher acknowledges the financial assistance of Arts Council England

Sir Winston Churchill Knew My Mother

Satyendra Srivastava

Here from Elsewhere

ÆB

Instead of a dedication

Poetry is a unique medium talking directly to anyone – heart to heart – and allowing one to share and invoke views and feelings. My chief concern when I start writing a poem is to aim for economy and clarity of language, to make every word count in conveying the message the poem contains or the picture it depicts.

After living in the West for so many years, I feel lucky to be able to express myself in two of mankind's greatest languages – English and Hindi. As a poet I try to keep an open mind to all cultures, places and religions. I try to express what it means to be human and to live in an ever-expanding world. I hope my poetry gives a flavour of the life of people in different cultures and places, and that my poems reflect people's inner life, their feelings and emotions.

Satyendra Srivastava
London, May 2006

Contents

Sir Winston Churchill Knew My Mother *(Hindi)* 2
Sir Winston Churchill Knew My Mother *(English)* 4
The Tree in Front of My Window 6
Albert Krishna Ali 9
Return to the Late Mr. Aiyer's Café 12
The Resolve 14
The Silent Beats of a Night Music 15
The Touch of the Monkey 16
Bob Shillington Plays Cricket Alone 17
Making Love in Common Waters 20
Ancestral Cobra 21
The Silent Buddha 22
Back to India 24
The Most Satisfying Moment 28
Making Krishna Redundant 29
The Nightingale Sings 30
Reliving Guernica 31
Anthem 32
Prajapati's Question 34
The Growth 35
The Creative Cell 36
In a Desolate Village 38
At an Asian Girl's Third Wedding 40
That Snake 42
Under the Rebels' Track 44
The Glacier Boy 46
Loser's Epitaph 48
A View of the World from a Half-Open Window 50
Reservoir 51

सर विंस्टन चर्चिल मेरी मां को जानते थे

सर विंस्टन चर्चिल जानते थे कि भारत क्या है
वे जानते थे
क्योंकि वे मानते थे कि भारत ब्रिटिश-साम्राज्य का
वह कोहिनूर हीरा है – जिसमें कभी सूर्य नहीं डूबता
सर विंस्टन जानते थे उस शहर को भी
जो उनके लोगों द्वारा, उन सब की सुविधा के लिए
हिमालय की गोद को काट कर, तराश कर
बनाया गया था – वह हिमानी शिखर-शिशु –
जिसे मसूरी शहर कहा जाता है
सर विंस्टन जानते थे कि वह कहां और क्यों है
क्योंकि वे, वहां उस उतार-चढ़ाव वाले
लंबे रास्ते पर सैर कर चुके थे
जो उन्हें ब्रिटिश-साम्राज्य के एक और
बेहद सुंदर शहर एडिनबरा के
प्रिंसेस-रोड की याद दिलाता था – कहीं किसी कोने से,
और सर विंस्टन यह भी जानते थे कि वहां
उस मसूरी शहर में भी,
ब्रिटेन के साम्राज्य की नींवों को खड़खड़ा देने वाली
कुछ ऐसी लहरें उठने लगी हैं,
जो भारतीय राष्ट्रीय संग्राम के
सिरफिरे नंगे फकीर का पागलपन ही उन्हें लग सकती थीं,
और सर विंस्टन यह भी जानते थे कि भारत में
उसी नंगे फकीर को पिता की तरह पूजने वाली
कुछ औरतों ने मसूरी शहर में भी रास्ते पर –
पंक्तियों में लेट कर
एक रोज, ब्रिटिश-साम्राज्य के सैनिकों के दस्तों को
आगे जाने से रोक दिया था
और उसमें कुछ थीं – ऐसी नारियां भी,
जिनके पेट फूले थे और जो
किसी भी क्षण अपने बच्चे को जन्म दे सकती थीं

इसीलिए, और बिल्कुल इसी कारण से लंदन पहुंचते ही
मैं हाइड-पार्क गेट गया था
और सर विंस्टन के बंद मकान के सामने खड़ा होकर,
सादर नमस्कार करके, यह जोर से कह पड़ा था -
सर विंस्टन आप मेरी मां को जानते हैं
वह भी एक सात महीने के बच्चे का पेट फुलाए
मेरे पिता का आशीष लेकर
मसूरी के उसी रास्ते पर लेट गई थी,
जहां से फौजियों के दस्तों को लौटना पड़ा था -

मैं उसी मां के पेट से जन्मा उसका बेटा हूं
और मेरा नाम सत्येन्द्र है
और मैं आपसे यह कहने आया हूं
कि मैं अब इंग्लैंड में आ गया हूं।

Sir Winston Churchill Knew My Mother

Sir Winston Churchill he knew India
He knew
Because India was to him the Kohinor
Of that Empire on which the sun never sets
Sir Winston also knew the town
Which his people had built for their comfort and ease
Cutting and carving it from the Himalaya's lap
– That child of the icy summits – that town
Which is called Mussoorie
Sir Winston knew where that town was and why
Because he had walked its long street rising and falling
Which had reminded him – somewhere somehow –
Of Princes Street in Edinburgh, another
Extremely beautiful town in the British Empire
And Sir Winston knew this too that
Also in the town called Mussoorie
A wave had risen
Shaking the foundations of Britain's Empire
The kind of wave that would seem to him
Just the folly of that crazy naked fakir of
India's national struggle
And Sir Winston knew this too that
In India some women who
Worshipped that same naked fakir as a father
Had laid down one day in the town of Mussoorie
In rows in the road and prevented the units
Of soldiers of the British Empire from going further
And among them had been some women who
Heavy with child could have given birth at any moment

Therefore exactly for this reason I
Went to Hyde Park Gate as soon as
I reached London
Stood in front of Sir Winston's shut house
Bowed respectfully, then spoke out loudly
'You, Sir Winston, knew my mother
Pregnant in her eighth month
Having received my father's blessing
She too laid down in
That road in Mussoorie
From where the army units had to return –
I am the son born from that mother's womb
And Satyendra is my name
And I have come to tell you
That I have now arrived in England.'

The Tree in Front of My Window

This tree in front of my window
changes throughout the seasons, but
does not change the way man changes.

To change with changing seasons
is its being.
I have seen on it
the varying joys and sorrows
of my life become history.
I have found myself dance
with the graceful movements of its leaves.
In wind and rain I have seen
the fearful storm within me
rage in its noise and prospect.
When the first rays of the sun fell on it
I have changed the page on my calendar.
When in it after midnight
the sound of distant bells fell quiet
then I have turned over
a still blank seeming underhandedly departed page
of a day in my life.
When all its leaves have fallen –
and the naked skeleton of branches began to show
then I have felt myself becoming
a stooping old man
but then whenever new leaves appeared on it it seemed to me
that I had been reborn
and as the leaves were growing
so grew my spirit
my body
and every vein of my life too.

When birds came flying
and took a perch
on its branches, some bent some tall
then I felt I was joining a vast world
and whenever the birds flew off again
then the transience of nearness shook me
and I understood the Mahabharata of loneliness.

In the shade of this tree I
have heard Krishna speak of love to Radha –
dancing gracefully to the sound of my flute.

Under this tree
I have also seen
T S Eliot's rage
as he rephrased his claims
to give them new force.

When an army at rest surrounded the tree
I shot its soldiers one by one as they were cleaning their rifles.
I have also heard various coarse jokes tried out on girls
and under this tree
I have found heaps of bodies
of rotting revolutionaries too.
I have seen
stuck to this tree advertisements, announcements
proclamations
suggesting that however clearly we see the world
it is still more than that
more beautiful more hideous
but however its condition we live inside it
fighting each our own battle.

Right under this tree I have seen
that all humanity
is crammed into a bus
and the conductor is shouting his head off
we are all on the moving bus, all of us
and if someone gets off this moving bus
he is a coward – a deserter.
Above this tree I have also seen
banners being planted
and taken down again
and sometimes also being torn to pieces.

This tree
is the horizon of my world
stretching endlessly
and sometimes it is also a staircase –
which goes nowhere.
This tree is the symbol of my timeless dreams
and the graveyard of all my thoughts
but most of all
this tree is my friend
who always stands in front of my window
and looks at me.

Albert Krishna Ali

Those who are walking with me
are
Albert Krishna Ali
Emerging from different houses
are
Albert Krishna Ali
Wearing on their foreheads, their cheeks and their lips
sandalwood marks of blessing
kisses of love
of a mother, a son or a daughter
are
Albert Krishna Ali
People who receive their tickets
with a scowl or a wry smile
from the white bus conductor
They are
Albert Krishna Ali
Where others sit in silence
hide their faces
behind their newspapers
pretend to see nothing
those sitting next to them
softly humming or singing film tunes
are
Albert Krishna Ali
To people in this country they are foreign millstones round their necks
they are those
who steal their salaries
lay claim to their pensions
pollute their schools
those whose alien ideas and culture penetrate their own
who spread the smell of spicy foods
They are
Albert Krishna Ali

They who are liked by factory managers
for working twelve hours at a time
doing the jobs
which are too boring or degrading
to attract Englishmen
They are
Albert Krishna Ali
They whose presence in large numbers
makes the natives move
to other areas
They are
Albert Krishna Ali
They who may be
the last to leave
They are
Albert Krishna Ali
They who with their children
suffer blows and knocks
and all kinds of hardship
yet toil with all their might
to give the children a better life
the best of educations
They are
Albert Krishna Ali
They who do not leave their old
until their time has come
and do not dump their parents
in an old people's home
in orphanages or asylums
They are
Albert Krishna Ali

Those who have different faiths
different beliefs, different ways of life
but whose skin colour
says what they are
and to the natives here
to their own neighbours
to the factory managers
they are just 'Pakis' and in Rushdie's context
'Musalman' or
to the older generation
'Gangadeen'
They are
Albert Krishna Ali
Oh my countrymen
Why fight amongst yourselves?
Trample or murder each other?
Cross the boundaries, you fools!
And look across
cast your eyes here
You will find
if your skin is not fair like the skin of whites
you are all Pakis
Niggers
and Muslims
May your name be
Albert
Krishna
or Ali

Return to the Late Mr. Aiyer's Café

In this neat corner
Of Lanka Varanasi
The evening is not the same today
Nor the winter smoke
The fillings in *dosas* are different too
Less coriander leaf
And mustard seed
But the chilli is sharper
So is the loneliness
And the roars of past silence

Where once was the unruly garden of the deity
Behind whose bushes Krishna played his hypnotic flute
And maids danced to his rhythm
Today harsh concrete and four story buildings
TV antennas and telephone wires
Crossroad signs
And the dreams lying on a high raised pavement
A corpse waiting to be carried forward
The procession in the making

Affection was once a ladder here
Every upward dream a game of indulgence
Everyone's searching eyes
Stories untold
Dreams actions with no holds barred
And Mr. Aiyer's café the land of karma

Now outside this air-conditioned environment
I see over the uncountable moving heads
A road stretching nowhere
And there is a pathway
Returning within me
To my unknown territory
Which could never draw a charted path
Now a memory
And on both sides of this memory lane
In front of the café
There is a new route to the temple

Where the beggars still sit
But now under the shade
And the priests chant for a better tomorrow

And here I am searching for myself
Once more where it all began
Long long ago
In Mr. Aiyer's café
Lanka Varanasi
My home town

The Resolve

I watch them
Singing the songs of love
Looking at their tattoos
All those names in them
The Catherines the Elizabeths
The Dianas and Margarets
And then I listen to them
Chanting *Rule Britannia*
And *Pakis go home*
I see them polishing their helmets
Oiling their knives
Demonstrating their kicks on a piece of brick
While looking at me
Etc etc etc
Yet I find myself
On every retreating day
Sitting in the same corner
In the coldest spot
With the resolve to survive
And I survive
And the next morning I get up
Wash
Offer my prayers and
Singing a popular hymn
Go to the shop
Open up the shutter
Switch on the lights
And look at the deposit books
And I feel satisfied
I smile pat my back
Well done son
You'll survive
And I do
And I stay
I hear some of them go
Down under

The Silent Beats of a Night Music

This steel is cold
The woods silenced
And the gut skin torn from the core
After a midnight wake

The last of the worshippers
Have left their candles
On the altar and walked away
Repenting
From now on their vow is never to utter a word
So this deathly silence
Invited every drop of innocence and piety

Could this be the night
Of a new birth
A melody from the raw virgin blood
An echoing passion
Of a new dictat

The incarnation of time
Knows no bounds
But always has a place and a rhythm
And followers
So the mystery of the night
Will know its beginning
When the silent beat of its music
Carves out its own message
And a new meaning
And a vision

The Touch of the Monkey

This is the day of the touch of the monkey
The kitchen fire burns
The tap water runs
The tiny hands of children reach out
To be lifted up and caressed

This is the day of the touch of the monkey
No woman is allowed to touch
Bathe cook pray or make love
This is the day of Eve's unwanted blood
Running down and draining away

This is the day of the touch of the monkey
Menstruation forbids her to take the world as it is
Or should be

In this lonesome night
When there is no one worth touching by a monkey
I feel that everything but everything
Is touched by it
Nothing can conceive
No seed can be sown
No penetration can relieve the pain of desire

On this day of the touch of the monkey
Oh my distant love
I still dream of a hand offering an apple
Of assurance
Because I am ready to sow the seed

Even on this day of the touch of the monkey
The man is ready as always
To suck the breeding point
Just to prove that the end has not come yet

Bob Shillington Plays Cricket Alone

Bob Shillington Plays Cricket Alone
Bob Shillington, whose white and grey hair is blown all
Over
Who wears three woollen coats even in the heat
Who has just got up from sleep
And just as he gets up
Takes up the bottle beside him though almost finished
Empties the wine left last night into his intestines
Then the cardboard box which is his bed and bedding
Folds, keeps it in a corner
Abuses one or two passers by
Now with the help of an unfinished wall
Is playing cricket
Bob Shillington in his hands
Takes a foot and a half long thin stick
Holding it firmly, moving it up and down, lifting it sky
High
Is now batting
Bob Shillington
Lifting his bat a little higher
Is shouting
Throw!
Bastards! Throw all
Throw one by one
Throw fast
Throw slow
Throw a googly
I will hit every ball
Hit each and every one of them
I will hit a four
Hit a sixer
Hit all
Hit each and every one!

Bob Shillington is shouting
And playing cricket
Bob Shillington is also feeling
That nobody is bowling
No-one is throwing the ball from any side
After a while
Bob Shillington keeps his bat by the stumps of the bricks
And observing the people coming and going
Sometimes he laughs
And sometimes abuses

Bob Shillington just saw an Asian
Bob Shillington stopped him
Asked him for money for tea
And was turned down with cool Asian politeness
The Asian went and Bob Shillington kept looking at him
Then he shouted
You son of a bitch!
Come unwanted here!
Eat our bread
And do not give us money!

Then Bob Shillington becomes quiet
And lifts his bat, offering it on all sides
Keeps batting
Keeps abusing
Bob Shillington abuses all
Except children
Boys sometimes throw stones, banana peel, or other things
At him
Or go near him
Keep their handkerchiefs to their noses
And spit on his smelly coat
Even then
Bob Shillington utters not a word
Only laughs
And when they go away
Then he shouts

All will go! When the time comes they will all go
All will pass unchanged
Just as Peter went, open-mouthed, hands flung
Used to call himself a captain before me
All will go, yes, yes, all will leave
As Hitler went, Stalin went
As major Livingston went
Wanted to bowl me out, the rascal, betrayer
As Maggie will go, Mother Teresa will go –
Came here calling London a Calcutta!

Like every day
Even today
Bob Shillington is playing cricket alone
Hitting hard and strong
Shouting loud and long, abusing
Throw!
Bastards throw!
Throw hard
Throw slow
Throw a googly
Throw
Throw with all your might!

Making Love in Common Waters

The point was not that they did not possess
Any social conscience
That all the looming threats
Of wars and conflicts
And the ever rising percentages
Of thefts rapes murders burglary
Did not touch them
It was also not
That they didn't give a shit who became president
Prime minister chancellor or martial law administrator
Of which country
Or of which principality
For them it was all a routine, clockwork
That all this had to be
That it is in the nature of things
That Man will commit crime
And make a mess
To survive
Also
However loudly the ideals are pronounced
And the leaders of men are given the task
Of cleaning up
And in order to do so
Machiavelli's prince is bound to emerge
So
When they had bribed the caretaker
To look the other way
And after all the swimmers had gone
They made love
In the common waters
They did not do it to satisfy their ego
That they were different
But they felt that by making love in the dirt of others
They were purifying the water
And themselves too

Ancestral Cobra

For the children of Nagpuri
The cobra did not have
Any ancestral value
Yet the womenfolk left
A bowl of sweet milk every night
Near the women's bathing place
And the children's curiosity
Took them at the crack of every dawn
To find out if the snakes had come
And drunk the milk
In the night
And after finding the milk still
Unconsumed they laughed
And taunted their mothers
Why do you waste milk like this, Ma?
There aren't any cobras now
They are all dead, history, kaput
My mother with wet tears
And rolling eyes thereupon would only say
My dearest you don't understand
You are not a mother
A mother knows the pain of carrying
A child in her womb for nine months
In this old village one mother
Carried a cobra baby as I carried you
That mother was bathing right there
A cobra passed by – she panicked
Folded her palms and prayed
O cobra, please don't hurt me
The cobra stood erect for a moment
And looked at her as if spellbound by her beauty
Spat out a white liquid that fell
Almost between her legs
Nine months later she gave birth to a cobra baby
In this family by providing milk
We say to the world that babies are babies
Human or cobra

The Silent Buddha

The good old Buddha
He witnessed them all
With his eyes closed
His feet Lotus-folded
His lips smiling
His palm blessing
Because he couldn't help
He was right there
Right in front
On the mantelpiece
He saw it all
With sure impassive face
The dance of shining firm round handsome hips
Creating havoc
On the mosaic of soft rug on the pucca floor
The fucks of a lifetime
He witnessed them all
With silence
All alone
Without clapping
Without bucking anybody up
So had seen in his life-time
Homeless men shivering and begging in streets
But perhaps not this one-night flip
A rich well dressed beautiful lady inviting a handsome
Young homeless boy to her home
On the floor
And the rug
To go into her everywhere
With the ever-increasing sound of the drum-beat
The hi-fi sound penetrating the sky and the sandalwood
Incense intoxicating every move

All that happened and happened so beautifully
So powerfully
Because the desire was there and the chance
The good old Buddha
No disrespect to you, sir
But I would say this
Desire is not the root of all troubles
In here it is of joy
And that can be anywhere
If the time is ripe
And the willingness is there
And the hunger is immense

Back to India

The students say –
they are going to India
they are going
not only to study, travel and see
but are going in order to find
that which is not found in their countries
they are going to this place
where the traditions,
customs and values of a thousand years
still count as the ideal
and are even today followed in everyday life.

The students went to India
because most old countries with an ancient civilisation
have seized upon change to such a degree
that their past
now only remains as museum exhibits:
like Egypt, where the splendour of the Pharaoh kings and queens
is far removed now from the life of the people
the inheritance of the vaults
and the great philosophers and thinkers of Greece
now only survive
as relics on the school curriculum.

The students said
that they were going to India
the place where it is said that
even the poor illiterate uneducated masses
still recall in their own plain tongues
their sages and saints, goddesses and gods, warriors and heroes
together with their sacred texts and devotional sentiments.

That is what the students said.

Now they have returned
now they say: India was not
as we thought.

It now seems to them that the people of India
do not perceive the inner power of their country
that those Indians who acquire a taste for money
bury the soul of their country in vaults
like the Pharaoh kings and queens
for them the Western world becomes the place
to follow and aspire
these people have become greater Western materialists
than the Western people themselves
and just like the Western people they don't ask questions
they simply accept.

Having returned the students also say
that in that country the poor are now so poor
that when they now recall
their sages and saints, legends and sacred texts
and their famous poets such as Surdas and Tulsi then
it is only repeating in parrot fashion what they have learnt
and without any real feeling
and people there put sacrificial bribes at the feet of
Lakshmi
as if they were earnings from hard work.

Having returned the students say
that everywhere these things
destroyed their whole romantic image
of India and its people, and
they did not think that this was a country
better than all others in the world
but still, having returned from India, so many students
now want to go back again.

Some say
they will go back and make completely sure
this time, once and for all,
that they did not misunderstand this country.
Some say
they will go back
because some people live there even now
who touching other human beings with their pure and holy soul
will transfer and set into motion a unique and growing power
so that from this one precious touch
their own gold may shine forth.

And then there are others: those who also want to go back there
because of the Himalayas
which, touching the heavens,
give perception and purity
and awaken even in the defeated and overburdened humans
a divine dignity.
No other such mountains exist.

Because however dirty the river Ganga has become
she will awake such hidden thoughts
which wash away all our inner sins –
during a time of self-examination
and then the Ganga does not just remain a dirty river
but she becomes the kind of current which
for centuries has taken everything away
which like the sins of time
enters her and remains within her.
The students want to go to India again
because still there are places like those *ghats* in Benares
where the entirety of life comes into view
before the eyes of those who still can simply see:
when you sit on the river on a boat
and look towards the *ghat*:
there to the left you see a crowd of people...
always on the move... growing... shrinking...
and sometimes there is laughter, sometimes there are tears
sometimes there is singing
and everywhere the eagerness for a full, complete life.

And to the right on Manikarnika Ghat
at some distance these different life stories end
in the funeral pyres
their scalp crackling.
Those wishing to return to India a second time
are this time not in search of the remarkable and strange
but they set out to find the essence of some
unity of life joining together piece by piece
all truth
they go to learn the truth because
they say in India there is still something
which though grown in the dirt
touches the heart somehow
just like a lotus!

The Most Satisfying Moment

It was the last glance
Of an immortal look
The touch of a dying
Gentle spark
The echo of a bursting glacier within
A silent cry
From a dried hollow throat
It was my mother's last thirst
The word *pani* only half uttered
I gently poured water from a spoon
She gulped a few drops
And tried to look again
Perhaps to bless me
Perhaps to tell me
How the last drop of life's nectar tasted
But she couldn't
A gasp
The water dropped back on her
Parched wounded lips
And she was gone
And I felt elevated
As never before
Quenching the last thirst
Is the most satisfying moment

Making Krishna Redundant

The bed like an island sleeps
The night half this side
Half merging into the mystery of what next stands
Under the blanket's silence there are sparks
Pushing the unheeded urges to limits
The smell of the fried flesh of desires
And the hyper sighs rising higher and higher
Like mushrooms shooting up in the Nevada desert
They replay the history of conquest
Robert Oppenheimer had said
It was the blast that brought him back to
Reality and Krishna
You can't compare a bed situation
With the nuclear testing ground I agree
But Mahabharata can be made and
Reduced to a mere concept here with no holds barred
And like Kama Sutra the urge to originality and creativity
Is ever ready to release the potential where
Even Krishna with all his Karma yoga
Could become redundant

The Nightingale Sings

She was told that the nightingale
Sings in Berkeley Square. She was
Told this by her English teacher and

The London-born Rakesh too. So the
Proposal of marriage was accepted
At once. Father was lured so was she.

House of her own in Belsize Park
Carpet wall to wall TV and Video
Dishwasher and tumble dryer and

What not. Newly wed Anjali left
The village for the promised land
And on arrival found the task of

Sharing. Working for the mortgage
Washing machine still to be paid for
A new life began in a department

Store in Oxford Street. And
While vacuuming the office and
Cleaning out the ladies' she

Looks across the street to Berkeley
Square humming to an Indian tune the words
The nightingale sings...

Reliving Guernica

Stumbling here
Eyes closed into the corridors of
A death trap villa of history
Is like... like living a mortuary experience
You feel you are being carried alive
Open eyed in a hearse into a journey unknown
I lived these moments right here
In the *Prado Madrid*
And could have gone on
Making a lone voyage through the tunnel
Of endless sequels of wars and conflicts
Death and destruction
But for the French girl standing nearby
Who broke the spell
With her loud question to her boyfriend
How far is the *Eiffel Tower* from Barcelona
Pablo darling?

Anthem

He wasn't depressed at all
Looked at the moving train
Threw away the crumpled paper
After opening his fist and measuring the palm
Took a deep sigh
And walked away
Turned back and watched her going
Took out the handkerchief from the pocket
Wiped the tears and hopped into the waiting bus

There isn't much to this story
Only a beginning was that they had
Met at a social security office
Collected their benefits and walked side by side
Across the common
Then at the bus stop the question popped out
My place or yours
It was hers
They had a good time
And now they parted as strangers
Without any hope
And no regrets

William Crossland while watching the times go by
Has seen it all before
People telling each other goodbye
Kissing again and again
Then meeting once more under the same old clock
Next to the ticket window

And this year has been good
Not too many delays
No strikes
No accidents
And thieves were caught and sentenced
No store went bankrupt
There is a lot to be thankful for
So said the vicar again today
To the passing commuters

And people are getting ready for the Christmas crackers
In this land of ours
There is a need to rewrite the anthem
A hymn for the homeless
Under a flag of fire

There is a future for all of us
What are we waiting for?

Prajapati's Question

In the beginning
A Hindu scripture says
The earth was quite bare
There existed neither plants nor trees
Prajapati – the lord of creatures –
The active creator and supporter of the universe
Asked himself once
How can I obtain descendants
And after torturing and mortifying himself
He eventually produced Agni – the fire
From his mouth
The fact that Agni was produced
Out of his mouth meant that he
Became a consumer of food
Now Prajapati thought that
Although he had produced a food consumer
Yet there was no food for him
And indeed on this earth
There was no edible object
Other then Prajapati himself
Prajapati again asked
In that case
Would not Agni eat him up...
This burning question
Has haunted man
Thereafter

The Growth

A head grows on my head
bigger than the last
with the chime of every morning bell
the time clock of my lagoon
rhymes blue
the narrator's voice echoes:

Ravana had ten heads
yet couldn't seduce Sita
abducted and in his custody.

I see a lone camel
walking through Nietzsche's desert
carrying a soul
and then stopping to change
into a wild lion
to hunt and rule
then a child is born
with a virgin vanity
to start the game of
blood and victory
and wars and conflicts
the on-going sequel...

The eyes in my heads
watch rejected men
desperately stopping every passer-by.
With torches in their hands
on a bright sunny day
they ask their question:
where is the god
show me where he is?

Their question burns
the flame snakes rise
and we watch:

the next century is waiting in the corridor.

The Creative Cell

It all makes sense Brassai
travelling through your lens of graffiti
Paris looking fresh in darks
almost friendly
I read in the lines and images
the abstract of a word which transcends boundaries
of what is and should be

Under the railway bridge
urinating on the graffiti of the broken
brick wall
the rejected man makes his own graffiti
wet and warm
He says I have nothing against
the man who drew the nude here
what makes me mad is the fact
that here in this condemned shit pit
we need bread more than flesh
The bearded man continues:
You know it is in corners like these when
people did graffiti of hungry faces
shouting for bread, they realised
the futility of their efforts
so they marched on Versailles

Some say that man's imagination sharpens
while answering nature's call
his creativity blossoms in abundance
and it is evident here in this public toilet
expressing joy and sufferings
terrors frustrations and
many deep psychological complexes
of unknown artists
in figures postures
slogans and icons
from INRI's holy cross to NF swastika
so much is scribbled here
that no space is left anymore
also no loo paper
is someone using it on the production line?
Then certainly
a masterpiece is in the making
or another Versailles

In a Desolate Village

The Sunrise was natural in the Eastern Sky
The Sun's chariot was
moving forward with
full speed grandeur
And in its light
falling on earth
the eyes of humans,
birds and beings opened
Munna Bhai Shah
Mohammed Patel
Sabita Ben and others
had begun to come out to
start their routine
and the determined task
children crying and laughing
singing the tunes of Jan-Gan and
Vaishnavjan
Jai Jawan Jai Kisan
Victory to Farmers and Soldiers

Then suddenly
the wheels of the Sun's chariot
began to rumble and got thrown off course
The course of nature turned its tide
Then
first the earth cracked
then trees, pillars, walls
Thresholds of houses burst and opened up
buildings trembled
cracks appeared in seconds on the roads
the astounded sky was
taken aback and watched
people running
people stumbling
people trembling
people crying and shouting

falling in agony
gasping for life
and within a moment
disappearing in the earth
and becoming dust
in a graveyard
the astounded sky saw it all
and is still gazing on

And today when I am standing
on the rubble of destruction
and devastation
I am motionless
gazing all around
I feel
that under the ground
even now some breaths are alive
that from underneath
someone is knocking
in every crack I see
the smoke rising
either the Sun's rays are burning
or some helpless woman is
burning her hairlocks
and making smoke rise
to draw attention

But here
reality has made the eyes stone
and the sensational touches
and salty breezes binding us
and the distant hilltops have
become the silent spectators
of this death ritual
and nature's revenge

At an Asian Girl's Third Wedding

Under the jasmine garlanded tent
And rose watered air humidifier
They were there to see Kirpal's daughter
Honourably married

In the reception
They talked
And drank
Talked about Somalias
Bosnias and Sudans
Described the dried up skeletons
The rapes of women
And the situation back home
Ayodhya and its cavity ridden stone pieces
They talked miles and oceans

They talked and the girl
In the next room was
Weighed down by the golden gifts
Honourably

It was the girl's third wedding
The first in the temple
The second in a London registry office
The third here in the vast reception room
The newsagent Kirpal's accountant watched
Noting down the expenses
On mortgage and bank loan

By midnight they had all left
Leaving behind heaps of food and drinks
And all those talks
Hunger in Somalia
And Bosnia and India
And Pakistan and Bangladesh

Once they left
Worn out women began
Clearing up the leftovers
And a third world nostalgia

That Snake

That snake was not poisonous
(Perhaps)
She suddenly appeared
Then at some distance became
Tensely erect in front of me
Frozen I kept looking at her
She stayed erect
Did not move at all nor sway
Nor strike at me
Nor show any enmity at all
Just kept looking

Some moments later
My mind and body relaxed
Somehow I felt reassured
Decided I shall not let myself die deathlessly
Therefore I also stretched my neck
And began to look back at her tensely just as she was
Looking at me
I studied her closely
Looked at her eyes
In them was lure
At her body
In it was tenderness
At her skin
In it was sparkle
At her mouth
In it was a cold secret
Then I looked all around her
And everything I saw was clear
Sharply focussed, stirring hidden challenges

Then some moments later
Hearing some light noises
She seemed alarmed, undecided but unsettled
Turned around
And went back to some other place

That snake was not poisonous
(Perhaps)
Oh how many days has it been since I saw her
So very many years
Which now seem like ages
But she stayed in the memory perhaps because
I never afterwards met anybody like her
Who could give my desire to live
Such all consuming purpose

Under the Rebels' Track

She was never to blame
She only knew how to give herself up intact
Wholesomely and with dignity
For her too it was
A period of intermission
A wait for that weekly train to pass by
The breeding session was still on
And around the bridge the washermen after
Beating the dirt out from garments
Had hung them on the twisted ropes upside down
Pointing their fingers at them they were
Telling their stories and pouring their venom out
T had hung the familiar tricoloured *kurta*
Upside down with his spit marks on the chest area
Resembling two bullet holes and said this was the bastard
Who
Raped my sister and got away with it
B had hung the yellow trousers shaping them like a
Guillotine
And pointing at the zip cried it is there that the minister
Will have
To witness his final sunset
His chosen hour for carnal accomplishment
C was most forthcoming with bloodthirsty eyes she was
Tearing up
The black sari of the mistress of the landlord who had lived
And worked as a procuress of women
For his stable-shaped harem and
She herself was one of them
At midday where the scent of fallen jasmine flowers lay
Heavy on the hot
Air after being trampled by the cows
The storytellers got up and shouted at the top of their
Voices

It's no good grumbling
This time let's do it
And they did it
The train came they threw the petrol bomb and blew it up
All the four compartments shattered into pieces
Passengers cattle goods and all
Then they looked at the river flowing as usual like a
Morning *raga*
Next to the crowds the fire brigades the police and the
Army
And life in the stable next door went on as usual
A young breeder coming shouting joyfully
This time we have done it
This breed is going to be the best of the lot
The unadulterated purebred world conquering
Indian stallions

The Glacier Boy

They kept in touch
Like Himalayan glaciers
Overspilling from mountain's topknot
Into the bosom of earth's tranquillity
Like the *papi pet*, the
Hungry stomach compels
The mortals to melt and move

They came down in water drips
Drop by drop
With parting tears and
Fell into the fat man's kingdom

The cold stream with
A rhythm and movement
Of its own
Then registered the undercurrents
The silent words
The motionless journeys
The commitments through lip-sealed interpreters
Clearly expressed
And silently understood

Our *bulla* – the hill-billy
To us children
The sturdiest worker
The dreamer the toy maker
The disciplinarian even the governor
Working for thirty rupees a month
Reflected the essence of glacier movements
He one day proudly announced
That he had become a daddy
How come?
Asked my naughty sister
You haven't seen her for two years

The *bulla* replied
Standing erect
But we correspond
Our words our silent messages –
Less said more understood –
Carefully inscribed by the letter writer
Have always been taken in well
Like the mountain river

My sister smiled
Quickly changed the subject
And exclaimed
Never mind
Here comes the new one
To share the burden of India's other
Eight hundred million
Let us rejoice
At the birth of our nation's
Glacier baby

Loser's Epitaph

Drums still beating
Though the orchestra has disappeared
And horses have galloped away
Yet the war is not declared

I have been warned again
You touch her once more
And Waterloo follows

My appetite has not shrunk yet
It is the childhood belly
That has kept on growing
Carving out tastier and tastier objects
Chew them satisfy the appetite
And want more

So what has changed now
After the two world wars
And numerous skirmishes
Did I lose my appetite
For winning altogether
Believing firmly
In war actually no one wins

It's the hunger of the craziest that grows and grows
And stretches from a field to the battleground
So this resignation
Has stifled me now
Without firing a single shot
I feel I am done

Mama had predicted
Whatever life brings you my pet
You will never be a coward
So why this indifference
Just because I have been warned again
Never to touch her

Now here I am like a French cavalier
Giving up the empire of Paris
To Nazis to trample upon
The greatest beauty of all

On the scale of nostalgia
I am some hundred years old now
As old as that Boulevard St Michel
Coffee house where Voltaire scribbled his doubts and hopes

So I tell people at large
And whomever it concerns particularly
I have not given up yet
Just waiting for her
To make the second most important move
In the meantime I stand in front of her portrait
Day and night
Keeping both my hands
In my trouser pockets
And think of England
Always a winner
At the end
Eventually

A View of the World from a Half-Open Window

Like the diplomacy of love
During the first meetings
The calculated words
The sideways grin with
Every smile
Half-projected commitments
With sips of something
Thoughts translating to
Controlled gazes into the future
Where dreams deposit
Their faith in a
Building Society account
I am looking at the world
From a half-open window
And enjoying it
Here
I hear no shouts
No comments
No media jerks
No regrets of
Wrongly typed texts
The world looks good today
With oceans of promises
I feel it's growing into me
Like a fragrance
Echoing like a symphony into
My veins and blood
I feel the presence of
Endless openings

I am falling in love
I want to sing today
In Sachmo's words
What a wonderful world

Reservoir

Time was
When he could
Relate to the symphony wholesomely
The higher the notes the faster the walkabout
Even the chasing the silent heartbeats
Speeding running like a hound after a plastic hare
Never to catch the tailend even
And then stopping and giving up
Expressed in the resigned distant looks
Resounding within like a subdued echo in the hall
After hanging up the instruments
The onlookers at every step watching every move intensely
And committed
Their applause never to die down
The music goes on and should
Now is the time
To draw up the balance sheet
Life's give and take
Though the orchestra has become smaller
Reducing itself first to a quartet
Then a trio
Then a duet and finally a solo
Life's melody of memory and nostalgia
And this too must go on
A musical extravaganza
Standing in the middle of the sweet memories of remembrance
And within the margins of all endeavours
He stands like all of us a solitary figure
Holding dearly the last cord of survival
Life itself
Sanctified and codified
Ever ready to be handed over
To the next messenger

Satyendra Srivastava was born in Azamgarh, Uttar Pradesh, India. He studied at the University of Poona from 1953–57, and the University of London from 1962–77, receiving his PhD in history in 1978. He lectured in Indian Studies at the University of Toronto from 1968–71 and at the University of Cambridge from 1980–2003.

With many published collections of poetry in Hindi, as well as plays for the stage and radio, he has also been a columnist for various Indian publications. He writes in both Hindi and English, although the poems in this collection were all written in English. Previous collections published in English are *Talking Sanskrit to Fallen Leaves* (Peepal Tree Press, 1995), *Between Thoughts* (Samvad, 1998) and *Another Silence* (Samvad, 2003).

Since retiring from Cambridge, Satyendra has travelled to many parts of the world to give lectures and read his poems: from the US, Japan and Russia to South Africa, Israel and Egypt, among many other countries. He has received several awards for his writing and published travelogues. He lives in London and Cambridge, and frequently travels back to India.

The title poem, *Sir Winston Churchill Knew My Mother*, was translated from English into Hindi by the author.

These poems have previously appeared in *Ambit*, *Iron*, *Poetry Digest*, *Verse* (UK and USA), *Nutshell*, *The Pathway*, *The Spectator*, *Smiths Knoll*, *Illuminations*, *Planet International*, *Hybrid*, *New Spokes*, *Exile*, *The Haiku Quarterly*, *Dial 174*, *Paris Atlantic*, *Trinidad Guardian*, *New Hopes International*, *Wasafiri*, *Quartos*, *Understanding*, *Poetry New Zealand*, *London Quarterly*, *What of Tomorrow* and *Indian Literature*. The author gratefully acknowledges the editors of these publications.